Cars & Trucks

This North American edition first published in 1986 by

Gareth Stevens, Inc.
7221 West Green Tree Road   Milwaukee, Wisconsin 53223, USA

Conceived, designed, and first produced in the United Kingdom with an original text copyright by Frances Lincoln Ltd.

Typeset by: Ries Graphics, ltd.
Series editor: Mark J. Sachner
Art direction and design: Debbie MacKinnon & Gary Moseley
Additional illustration/design: Laurie Shock

Library of Congress Cataloging-in-Publication Data

Thompson, Graham, 1940-
    Cars & trucks.

    (Wheels)
    Includes index.
    Summary: Illustrations and simple text introduce the characteristics and uses of a variety of cars and trucks.
    1. Automobiles—Juvenile literature.   2. Trucks—Juvenile literature. [1. Automobiles.
2. Trucks] I. Title. II. Title: Cars and trucks. III. Series: Thompson, Graham, 1940-   Wheels.
TL147.T48   1986   629.2′222   86-5702

ISBN 1-55532-125-9
ISBN 1-55532-100-3 (lib. bdg.)

Cars
& Trucks

Graham Thompson

Gareth Stevens Publishing
Milwaukee

Rolls Royce

The Rolls Royce is a fancy car made in England. It has a big engine. And it costs lots of money.

Police Car

Police cars are on the lookout for trouble. They have sirens and flashing lights. These warn cars to clear the way.

8

Ambulance

Ambulances also have sirens and flashing lights. They take people who are hurt or sick to the hospital.

Fire Engine

Fire engines race to put out fires. With their long hoses and ladders, they save people from danger.

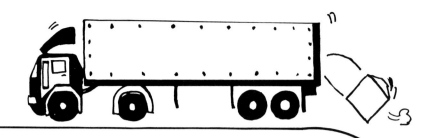

Tractor Trailer

Tractor trailers are also called semis. Semis take things from one place to another.

The back is called a semitrailer. It is very long. Can you count the tires?

14

The cabs are also called tractors. They are shiny and bright. Look at all the lights on this one!

Tow Truck

Tow trucks have sturdy bodies. They also have long chains. Has your car ever been towed away?

Four-wheel-drive Vehicle

This car is powered by all four wheels. It is perfect for places where other cars get stuck.

Car Transporter

Car transporters take cars from the factory to the showroom.

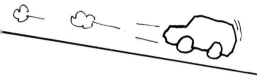

How do the cars get on and off?
And how do they stay in place?

Bus

Buses carry many people at once. Some buses go across town. But others may travel thousands of miles!

Index of Cars and Trucks